# First World War
and Army of Occupation
# War Diary
France, Belgium and Germany

59 DIVISION
178 Infantry Brigade,
Brigade Trench Mortar Battery
13 February 1917 - 30 November 1918

WO95/3025/13

The Naval & Military Press Ltd
www.nmarchive.com
Published in association with The National Archives

Published by

## The Naval & Military Press Ltd

Unit 10 Ridgewood Industrial Park,

Uckfield, East Sussex,

TN22 5QE England

Tel: +44 (0) 1825 749494

www.naval-military-press.com

www.nmarchive.com

*This diary has been reprinted in facsimile from the original. Any imperfections are inevitably reproduced and the quality may fall short of modern type and cartographic standards.*

© **Crown Copyright**
**Images reproduced by permission of The National Archives, London, England, 2015.**

# Contents

| Document type | Place/Title | Date From | Date To |
|---|---|---|---|
| Heading | WO 3025 59th 1781b 178th Lt Trench Mortar Bty 1917 Apr-1918 Nov 1917 Feb & Mar Also | | |
| Heading | 59th Division 178th Infy Bde 178th Lt Trench Mortar Bty Apr 1917-Nov 1918 | | |
| Heading | War Diary 178 Light Trench Mortar Battery February 1917 | | |
| War Diary | Hurdcott Wib | 13/02/1917 | 13/02/1917 |
| War Diary | Southampton | 24/02/1917 | 24/02/1917 |
| War Diary | Havre | 26/02/1917 | 27/02/1917 |
| War Diary | Longueau | 28/02/1917 | 28/02/1917 |
| Heading | War Diary Of 178 Infantry Brigade Light Trench Mortar Battery From 1-3-1917 To 31-3-1917 Inclusive (Volume 2) | | |
| War Diary | Longueau | 01/03/1917 | 01/03/1917 |
| War Diary | Warfusee-A | 01/03/1917 | 09/03/1917 |
| War Diary | Foucaucourt | 09/03/1917 | 14/03/1917 |
| War Diary | Trenches | 16/03/1917 | 16/03/1917 |
| War Diary | Foucaucourt | 20/03/1917 | 20/03/1917 |
| War Diary | Trenches | 20/03/1917 | 20/03/1917 |
| War Diary | Belloy | 24/03/1917 | 24/03/1917 |
| War Diary | Villers-Carbonel | 24/03/1917 | 26/03/1917 |
| War Diary | Athies Wood | 26/03/1917 | 28/03/1917 |
| War Diary | Bouvincourt | 28/03/1917 | 28/03/1917 |
| Heading | War Diary Of 178 Light Trench Mortar Battery For Month Of April 1917 Vol 2 | | |
| War Diary | Bouvincourt | 01/04/1917 | 01/04/1917 |
| War Diary | Flechin | 01/04/1917 | 01/04/1917 |
| War Diary | Before Le Verguier | 06/04/1917 | 07/04/1917 |
| War Diary | Flechin | 09/04/1917 | 19/04/1917 |
| War Diary | In The Line | 22/04/1917 | 29/04/1917 |
| War Diary | War Diary Of 178 Light Trench Mortar Battery For The Month Of May 1917 Vol II | | |
| War Diary | Hesbecourt | 01/05/1917 | 06/05/1917 |
| War Diary | Vraignes | 07/05/1917 | 29/05/1917 |
| War Diary | Hamelet | 30/05/1917 | 30/05/1917 |
| Miscellaneous | Operation From 19-4-17 To 6-5-17 | 19/04/1917 | 19/04/1917 |
| Miscellaneous | 178 L.T.M.B Operation Order No 3 | 03/05/1917 | 03/05/1917 |
| Map | Hargicourt | | |
| Heading | War Diary Of 178 Light Trench Mortar Battery For The Month Of June 1917 Vol II | | |
| War Diary | Equancourt | 01/06/1917 | 01/06/1917 |
| War Diary | Metz-En-Couture | 01/06/1917 | 01/06/1917 |
| War Diary | Metz | 01/06/1917 | 11/06/1917 |
| War Diary | Metz-En-Couture | 11/06/1917 | 11/06/1917 |
| Heading | 178th Light French Mortar Battery July To December 1917 | | |
| Heading | War Diary Of 178 Light Trench Mortar Battery For Month Of July 1917 Vol II | | |
| War Diary | Vaux-En Amienois | 03/07/1917 | 03/07/1917 |
| War Diary | Peronne | 03/07/1917 | 04/07/1917 |

| War Diary | Line | 05/07/1917 | 09/07/1917 |
| War Diary | Dessart Wood | 09/07/1917 | 09/07/1917 |
| War Diary | O35d53 | 13/07/1917 | 13/07/1917 |
| Heading | War Diary Of 178 Light Trench Mortar Battery For The Month Of August 1917 Vol II | | |
| War Diary | Camp In 035d | 01/08/1917 | 24/08/1917 |
| War Diary | Aveluy | 24/08/1917 | 29/08/1917 |
| War Diary | Godwaersvelde | 31/08/1917 | 31/08/1917 |
| War Diary | 178th Inf Bde Light T.M Battery War Diary For September 1917 | | |
| War Diary | Farm J1a29 (Sheet 27) | 03/09/1917 | 20/09/1917 |
| War Diary | L13 G 8.8 | 23/09/1917 | 23/09/1917 |
| War Diary | Bedouin Camp | 24/09/1917 | 24/09/1917 |
| War Diary | Farm J1a 2.9 | 12/09/1917 | 12/09/1917 |
| War Diary | In The Line | 25/09/1917 | 25/09/1917 |
| War Diary | Schuller Galleries | 26/09/1917 | 27/09/1917 |
| War Diary | St. Jean | 29/09/1917 | 29/09/1917 |
| War Diary | Vlamertinghe | 29/09/1917 | 29/09/1917 |
| War Diary | War Diary Of October 1917 178th Light Trench Mortar Battery | | |
| War Diary | Vlamertinghe | 01/10/1917 | 01/10/1917 |
| War Diary | Boeseghem | 04/10/1917 | 04/10/1917 |
| War Diary | Wittes | 06/10/1917 | 06/10/1917 |
| War Diary | Coyecque | 06/10/1917 | 10/10/1917 |
| War Diary | Sachin | 11/10/1917 | 11/10/1917 |
| War Diary | Camblain Chatelain | 12/10/1917 | 12/10/1917 |
| War Diary | Barlin | 13/10/1917 | 13/10/1917 |
| War Diary | Petit Servins | 16/10/1917 | 22/10/1917 |
| War Diary | In The Line | 23/10/1917 | 31/10/1917 |
| Heading | 178th Light T.M.B November 1917 | | |
| War Diary | In Line Avion Sector | 01/11/1917 | 07/11/1917 |
| War Diary | Gouy Servins | 14/11/1917 | 14/11/1917 |
| War Diary | Etrun | 19/11/1917 | 19/11/1917 |
| War Diary | Hendecourt | 20/11/1917 | 20/11/1917 |
| War Diary | Gomiecourt | 23/11/1917 | 23/11/1917 |
| War Diary | Equancourt | 29/11/1917 | 29/11/1917 |
| War Diary | Trescault | 01/12/1917 | 01/12/1917 |
| War Diary | Bertincourt | 20/12/1917 | 20/12/1917 |
| War Diary | Barastre | 23/12/1917 | 23/12/1917 |
| War Diary | Beaulencourt | 25/12/1917 | 25/12/1917 |
| Heading | 178th Light T.M.B War Diary January 1918 | | |
| War Diary | Moncheaux | 08/01/1918 | 08/01/1918 |
| War Diary | Ambines | 19/01/1918 | 19/01/1918 |
| War Diary | Moncheaux | 28/01/1918 | 30/01/1918 |
| War Diary | War Diary For February 1918 178th Light Trench Mortar Battery | | |
| War Diary | Moncheaux | 01/02/1918 | 08/02/1918 |
| War Diary | Barly | 09/02/1918 | 09/02/1918 |
| War Diary | Boisleux St Mark | 10/02/1918 | 10/02/1918 |
| War Diary | Mory | 11/02/1918 | 11/02/1918 |
| War Diary | In The Line | 14/02/1918 | 02/03/1918 |
| War Diary | Mory | 10/03/1918 | 10/03/1918 |
| War Diary | In The Line | 21/03/1918 | 21/03/1918 |
| War Diary | Ayette | 22/03/1918 | 22/03/1918 |
| War Diary | Senlis | 25/03/1918 | 25/03/1918 |
| War Diary | Bavelincourt | 26/03/1918 | 26/03/1918 |

| | | | |
|---|---|---|---|
| War Diary | Fieffes | 28/03/1918 | 28/03/1918 |
| Miscellaneous | Ref. Sheets 51b S.W & Sheet 570 N.W. | | |
| Miscellaneous | Copy of Letter From Captain H.P.Greaves (Commdg. 178th L.T Mortar Battery) To Br.-General T.W. Stansfield. | | |
| War Diary | Cambligneul | 01/04/1918 | 30/04/1918 |
| War Diary | Houtkerque | 05/05/1918 | 05/05/1918 |
| War Diary | Stomer | 07/05/1918 | 07/05/1918 |
| Heading | War Diary Of 178th L.T.M Battery From 24th June 1918 To 30th June 1918 Volume I | | |
| War Diary | Fontaine-Les-Boulans | 24/06/1918 | 27/07/1918 |
| War Diary | Barly | 27/07/1918 | 31/07/1918 |
| Heading | War Diary Of 178th Light Trench Mortar Battery August 1918 | | |
| War Diary | Barly | 01/08/1918 | 02/08/1918 |
| War Diary | Blairville | 02/08/1918 | 17/08/1918 |
| War Diary | Barly | 18/08/1918 | 21/08/1918 |
| War Diary | Blairville | 21/08/1918 | 23/08/1918 |
| War Diary | Saulty | 24/08/1918 | 24/08/1918 |
| War Diary | Ham-En-Artois | 25/08/1918 | 27/08/1918 |
| War Diary | St Venent | 28/08/1918 | 31/08/1918 |
| Heading | War Diary Of 178th L. Trench Mortar Battery September 1918 | | |
| Miscellaneous | To The Head Quarters 178th Infantry Brigade | | |
| War Diary | Calonne-Sur La-Lys | 01/09/1918 | 02/09/1918 |
| War Diary | Lestrem | 03/09/1918 | 05/09/1918 |
| War Diary | Laventie | 06/09/1918 | 30/09/1918 |
| Heading | War Diary Of 178 Light Trench Mortar Battery for October 1918 | | |
| Miscellaneous | To Headquarters 178th Infantry Brigade | | |
| War Diary | Laventie | 30/09/1918 | 01/10/1918 |
| War Diary | Riez Bailleul | 01/10/1918 | 02/10/1918 |
| War Diary | Erquinghem-Lys | 03/10/1918 | 10/10/1918 |
| War Diary | Bois Grenier | 10/10/1918 | 15/10/1918 |
| War Diary | Mont Pindo | 16/10/1918 | 16/10/1918 |
| War Diary | Lomme | 17/10/1918 | 17/10/1918 |
| War Diary | Mons-En-Baroeul | 18/10/1918 | 18/10/1918 |
| War Diary | Forest | 19/10/1918 | 19/10/1918 |
| War Diary | Willems | 20/10/1918 | 20/10/1918 |
| War Diary | Templeuve | 21/10/1918 | 31/10/1918 |
| Heading | War Diary Of 178th L. Trench Mortar Battery November 1918 | | |
| War Diary | Templeuve | 01/11/1918 | 07/11/1918 |
| War Diary | Epinette | 08/11/1918 | 08/11/1918 |
| War Diary | Fauchy | 09/11/1918 | 09/11/1918 |
| War Diary | Anvaing | 10/11/1918 | 11/11/1918 |
| War Diary | Velaines | 12/11/1918 | 14/11/1918 |
| War Diary | Willems | 16/11/1918 | 16/11/1918 |
| War Diary | Petit Ronchin | 17/11/1918 | 30/11/1918 |

WO 3025
58th 17th18

178th Lt Trench
Mortar Bty

1917 Apr - 1918 Nov

1917 Feb + Mar also

1917

59TH DIVISION
178TH INFY BDE

178TH LT TRENCH MORTAR BTY
(Feb + Mar 17)
APR 1917-NOV 1918

CONFIDENTIAL

War Diary

178 Light Trench Mortar Battery

February 1917

Army Form C. 2118.

# WAR DIARY
## INTELLIGENCE SUMMARY.
(Erase heading not required.)

Instructions regarding War Diaries and Intelligence Summaries are contained in F.S. Regs., Part II. and the Staff Manual respectively. Title pages will be prepared in manuscript.

TRENCH MORTAR BATTERY  178th INFANTRY BRIGADE  59th DIVISION  B.E.F

FEBRUARY 1917.

| Hour, Date, Place | | Summary of Events and Information | Remarks and references to Appendices |
|---|---|---|---|
| 11.30 a.m, 13-2-17, | HURDCOTT, Wils | Inspected by H.M the King. Marched Past in Column of Route | |
| 7.30 p.m, 24-2-17, | SOUTHAMPTON | Embarked on SS "KARNAK" | |
| 11.30 a.m, 26-2-17 | HAVRE | Disembarked & proceeded to No.1 Rest Camp. | |
| 6.20 a.m, 27-2-17 | HAVRE | Left No.1 Rest Camp & entrained. | |
| 3-0 a.m, 28-2-17 | LONGUEAU | Detrained, & proceeded to Billets. | |

R.N. Pratt CAPT.
OC 178th Light Trench Mortar Battery.

Confidential.

## WAR DIARY
### of
### 178th Infantry Brigade LIGHT TRENCH MORTAR BATTERY.

from 1-3-1917 to 31-3-1917 inclusive.

(VOLUME 2)

Army Form C. 2118.

# WAR DIARY
## or
## INTELLIGENCE SUMMARY.
*(Erase heading not required.)*

Instructions regarding War Diaries and Intelligence Summaries are contained in F. S. Regs., Part II. and the Staff Manual respectively. Title pages will be prepared in manuscript.

LIGHT TRENCH MORTAR BATTERY - 178th INFANTRY BRIGADE.

MARCH, 1917.

| Hour, Date, Place | Summary of Events and Information | Remarks and references to Appendices |
|---|---|---|
| LONGUEAU. 1/3/17 - 9 a.m. | Left by Route March for Warfusee- Abancourt. | Ref |
| WARFUSEE-A. 1/3/17 - 1:30 p.m. | Arrived and took over Billets. H.Q. 15 Rue D'Amiens. | Ref |
| WARFUSEE-A 9/3/17 - 8:50 a.m. | Left by Route March for Foucaucourt | Ref |
| FOUCAUCOURT 9/3/17 - 11:15 a.m. | Arrived and took over Billets. H.Q. M 31 B 19 Map Ref 62 c SW | Ref |
| do 14/3/17 - 5:30 p.m. | Capt R.S. Pratt, 2nd Lt A.Q. Dickson, and 10 other ranks proceeded to left Sector of Dinnaware Front, from N 28 D 94 to T 4 O 76 (Map Ref. 62 c SW), for instructional purposes. | Ref |
| TRENCHES 16/3/17 6:30 p.m. | Left Trenches and returned to Battery H.Q. at Foucaucourt. | Ref |
| FOUCAUCOURT 20/3/17 - 3:30 p.m. | Battery left by Route March to relieve 177th Brigade T.M.B. in Left Sector of Dinnaware Front. Battery H.Q. Belloy. N 27 A 77. (Map Ref 62 c SW). | Ref |
| TRENCHES 20/3/17 6-0 p.m. | Relief executed. | Ref |

Army Form C. 2118.

# WAR DIARY
## or
## INTELLIGENCE SUMMARY.
(Erase heading not required.)

Instructions regarding War Diaries and Intelligence Summaries are contained in F. S. Regs., Part II. and the Staff Manual respectively. Title pages will be prepared in manuscript.

LIGHT TRENCH MORTAR BATTERY — 178th INFANTRY BDE.

MARCH 1917

| Hour, Date, Place | | Summary of Events and Information | Remarks and references to Appendices |
|---|---|---|---|
| BELLOY | 24/3/17 - 3.30pm | Battery left by Route March and proceeded to Villers-Carbonel | |
| VILLERS-CARBONEL | 24/3/17 - 5.0pm | Arrived and took over quarters. H.Q N36c35 (M.R. 62c SW). | |
| do | 26/3/17 - 6.0pm | Left by Route March & proceeded to ATHIES WOOD. | |
| ATHIES WOOD | 26/3/17 - 7.30pm | Arrived & took over quarters. H.Q. O35.B.38 (M.R 62c S W). | |
| do | 28/3/17 - 9.am | Left by Route March & proceeded to Bouvincourt. | |
| BOUVINCOURT | 28/3/17 - 11am | Arrived and took over quarters H.Q. M35 Bouvincourt – Beauvoir Road. | |

R.A. Pratt  CAPT.
COMMDG. 178 BDE, TRENCH MORTAR BATT.

CONFIDENTIAL

War Diary

of

178 Light Trench Mortar Battery

for

Month of April 1917

Vol 2

# WAR DIARY

**LIGHT TRENCH MORTAR BATTERY, 178th INFANTRY BRIGADE**

## INTELLIGENCE SUMMARY.
(Erase heading not required.)

Instructions regarding War Diaries and Intelligence Summaries are contained in F.S. Regs. Part II. and the Staff Manual respectively. Title pages will be prepared in manuscript.

LIGHT TRENCH MORTAR BATTERY - 178TH INFANTRY BRIGADE - 59TH DIVISION - B.E.F.

| Hour, Date, Place | Summary of Events and Information | Remarks and references to Appendices |
|---|---|---|
| BOUVINCOURT - 1/4/17 - 9-30 P.M. | Proceeded by Route March to FLECHIN | |
| FLECHIN - 1/4/17 - 11.0p.m. | Arrived & took over quarters HQ Q17A4 (M.R. 62c S.E) | |
| BEFORE LE VERGUIER 6/4/17 to 7/4/17 | On the night of the 6th-7th, 2 guns under 2nd Lieut H P GREAVES and 2nd Lt A A DICKSON assisted in a demonstration against LE VERGUIER while the latter was being attacked by the infantry from the south. No 1 Gun was positioned in an old German trench at L.33 C 9.2 - No 2 Gun in a trench at R3a9.4. Shots were fired from both guns into THIERRU COPSE. After the attack the guns were withdrawn. (Map Ref 62c N.E. & S.E). | |
| FLECHIN - night of 9-10/4/17. | 178th Infantry Brigade withdrawn into Reserve, Trench Mortar Battery remaining at FLECHIN. | |
| do. 10/4/17 - 12 Noon | Battery relieved 177th Inf Bde Light T.M.B in the line. HQ at HESBECOURT Part. 4 Guns on Main Line of Resistance at L16a45, L16a.65, L10c4, L10c.4½. | |
| IN THE LINE Night of 22-23/4/17 | 2 New emplacements constructed on Main Line of Resistance at L16c3.2, L16.2.3½ respectively. | |
| do. Night of 27-28/4/17 | One gun placed in position at VILLERET, L12c2.7. | |
| do. do. 28-29/4/17 | One gun do do do at L5.6.8½.3½. | |

G.A. Pratt CAPT,
COMMDG. 178 BDE. TRENCH MORTAR BATT.

CONFIDENTIAL

WAR DIARY
of
178 Light Trench Mortar Battery
for month of
MAY 1917

Vol II

Army Form C.

# WAR DIARY
## or
## INTELLIGENCE SUMMARY.
*(Erase heading not required.)*

Summary of Events and Information for month of May 1917

LIGHT TRENCH MORTAR BATTERY:- 178 Inf Bde 59 Div

Instructions regarding War Diaries and Intelligence Summaries are contained in F.S. Regs., Part II. and the Staff Manual respectively. Title pages will be prepared in manuscript.

| Hour, Date, Place | | Remarks and references to Appendices |
|---|---|---|
| 1-5-17 | Battery in the Line | For details see Special Reports, Map, and Operation orders attached |
| HESBECOURT 9 pm 6-5-17 | Battery relieved by the 176 Light Trench Mortar Battery, Proceeded by march route to VRAIGNES | Ref |
| VRAIGNES 7-5-17 to 29-5-17 | Daily training carried out while in rest. | Ref. |
| VRAIGNES 11-5-17 | 2nd Lt A.A. DICKSON proceeded to IV Army School of Mortars at VAUX-EN-AMIENOIS returning on 23-5-17 | Ref. |
| VRAIGNES 5 am 29-5-17 | Proceeded by march route to HAMELET | Ref |
| HAMELET 6.15 am 30-5-17 | Proceeded by march route to EQUANCOURT | Ref |

R.R. Pratt CAPT.
COMMDG. 178 BDE. TRENCH MORTAR BATT.

LIGHT TRENCH
MORTAR BATTERY,
178TH INFANTRY BDE.
No........
Date........

LIGHT TRENCH
MORTAR BATTERY,
178TH INFANTRY BDE.

No..........
Date..........

Report on Operations from 19-4-17
to 6-5-17

Ref Maps:-
62 C NE
62 B NW
Special Map

During the morning of 19-4-17 the 178 Light Trench Mortar Battery relieved the 177 Light Trench Mortar Battery with Headquarters in HESBECOURT and four guns behind the main line of resistance running through L.33, L.27, L.21, L.16 and L.10 (Sheet 62 C NE).

These guns were situated at about:-
  (1) L 16 a 40.50
  (2) L 16 a 45.50
  (3) L 10 c 70.10
  (4) L 10 c 70.05

Two guns were held in reserve at Headquarters, the remaining two being at the School.

From 19-4-17 to 6-5-17 the above positions were improved by digging a communication trench between Nos 1 and 2 guns and the construction of dugouts and ammunition recesses. Two further emplacements were also constructed behind the main line of resistance at about L 16 C 30.24 and L 16 C 30.15

On the night of 27/28 April after the attack on COLOGNE FARM and the QUARRY in L 5 d, at the request of the 2/6 Notts & Derby Regt a gun was placed in position at L 12 c 2.7. to protect the right flank of the above regiment and cover the valley in L 12 a and the sunken road. This position was purely defensive and the gun was not fired.

During the night of 28/29 April one gun was placed in position at L 5 b 85.35 to support the bombing block which had been established at L 5 b 9.4 by

by
the 2/8 Notts and Derby Regt on the night of 27/28 April. This gun was registered on the continuation of the old German front line trench in L5b at a range of 150 yards with yellow cartridge.

During the night of 29/30 April one gun was moved from the main line of resistance and placed in position at L5b 85.55. It was registered on a new German trench (NEW TRENCH) in L6a which was known to be held, at a range of 360 yards. During the same night bursts were fired at the junction of NEW Trench with the continuation of the old German front line trench in L6a [ENFILADE TRENCH]. At 7.45 pm 1-5-17 twelve rounds were fired at NEW TRENCH and seven direct hits were obtained. Parties of men were observed to run away along the trench.

At 6 pm 2/5/17 another gun was moved from the main line of resistance and placed at L5 67.4 in a shell hole deepened and improved to make an emplacement. This gun was registered on the UNNAMED FARM at the cross roads at L6a 10.

During the night of 2/3 May a bombing party covered by our mortars pushed forward and erected a permanent block at the point where the ENFILADE trench meets the sunken road at about L6a 15.45. A number of enemy bombs at the junction of ENFILADE trench and NEW trench were destroyed by our Stokes fire at the same time.

During the same night the gun from L12 c27 was advanced and dug in on the lip of the QUARRY at L5d 8.4 to fire on COLOGNE FARM in support of the attack on the following night. The men of the battery not in the line acted as a carrying party for ammunition for this gun.

An advanced ammunition dump was formed under the quarry bank at L 10 a 4.6.

On the night of 3/4 May the 2/5 Notts & Derby Regt.

Regt.

attacked COLOGNE FARM and MALAKOFF FARM and the officers of the 178 LTMB took command in the line as per attached copy of Operation Order No 5.

During the attack all guns fired as per above order with good effect.

On the right where the attack failed to reach its objective the retirement from Nomans land was covered by the gun under 2nd Lieut A A DICKSON; the men of the Battery not in the line carried up a further supply of ammunition to this gun.

The attack on the left was successful and both objectives were taken. Heavy enemy casualties were observed in NEW trench next morning due to our stokes fire

At 6 am 4-5-17 2nd Lieut H P GREAVES was withdrawn from the left sector into rest billets, leaving 2nd Lieut (?) B BOYS in command of the three guns.

Throughout the 4th May NEW trench was kept under observation and several enemy working parties were shelled and dispersed. At 10 am a sniper was located at L6 b 15.95 and killed by our fire.

During the afternoon the farm at L 6 a 1.0 was shelled with 10 rounds and then occupied by a post from the 2/8 Notts and Derby Regt.

At 9 pm 4-5-17 the enemy put down a very heavy barage of all varieties of shell from L 5 b 9.0 to F 29 d 9.0. and made a counter attack on the positions gained by us the previous night. The post at L 6 a 1.0 was compelled to withdraw and our men EAST of MALAKOFF FARM driven in. During the retirement an enemy machine gun was observed to be firing from the junction of NEW trench and ENFILADE trench. This was blown up by a stokes shell.

During the night of 5/6 an intermittent bombardment of the Unnamed farm and NEW trench was kept up by our mortars.

At 12.30 pm 5-6-17 our Machine Gunners reported an enemy machine gun at L6C52 firing at an aeroplane. The gun under 2/Lt Dickson was brought into action and direct hits obtained. The machine gun was observed to be completely destroyed.

During the night of the 5/6 May 2/Lt Dickson moved his gun to a position at about L5d9.1 and at 3.45 am 6-5-17 rapid fire was opened on the German trench at L12 a 2.8 where new earth had been noticed. A working party was caught by our fire and several casualties inflicted. In the morning the trench was observed to have been greatly damaged.

During the whole of the above operations approximately 325 Stokes shells were fired.

The accuracy of shooting was good.

Very few miss fires occured and as far as could be observed only 3 shells failed to explode during the whole time.

At 9 pm 6-5-17 the Battery was relieved by the 176 Light Trench Mortar Battery

In the Field
7-5-17

R. S. Pratt
_____ CAPT.
COMMDG. 178 BDE. TRENCH MORTAR BATT.

SECRET                                                                Copy N° 3
              178 LTMB OPERATION ORDER N° 3
Ref Maps 62c NE
         62b NW                                         3rd May '17

1. On the night of 3/4 the 2/5 Sherwood Foresters will attack and capture COLOGNE Fm and MALAKOFF Fm.

2. For the attack on COLOGNE there will be two objectives
   (a) Trench SW of Fm from L6c52 to L6c26
   (b) Trench immediately E of Fm from L6c64 to L6c57
   Blocks will be formed on right and left.
   The 2/8 Sr will get in touch with left by bombing up trench running N and S through L5b and L6c.

3. For the attack on MALAKOFF Fm there will be two objectives
   (i) Trench W of Fm. from L6a28.55 to F30c38.25
   (ii) Road on NE side of Fm from F30c91 to F30c7045

4. The 178 LTMB will assist by bombarding COLOGNE Fm and NEW TRENCH in L6a.

5. N° 1 gun in position at L5d94 and N°s 2,3,4 guns in old German front line trench in L5b.

6. 2/LT A.A. DICKSON will command N° 1 Gun and will be in position by 10.30 pm and will register at Zero – 30 on COLOGNE Fm buildings and Road at L6c46.
   At Zero + 3 rapid fire will be opened on Fm.
   At Zero + 6 fire will lift to above Road
   At Zero + 8 bombardment will cease and team will stand by to act as may be necessary.
   N°s 2 & 3 guns will be commanded by 2/LT H.P. GREAVES and will registered by daylight under 2/LT C D B BOYS. They will be set at 10 yds over range.
   From Zero to Zero + 8 N° 2 will bombard NEW trench L6a53 to L6a50.35 with rapid fire and N° 3 gun will bombard junction of same trench with ENFILADE trench to L6a50.35. At Zero + 8 both guns will cease fire and prepare to act as may be necessary.
   N° 4 gun will be commanded by 2/LT C D B BOYS and will register during daylight.
   From Zero to Zero + 4 it will bombard junction of NEW trench with ENFILADE trench. At Zero + 4 it will lift and bombard along ENFILADE trench. At Zero + 8 it will cease fire and prepare to move as may be necessary.

7. Remainder of Battery less Q'M Sgt and 1 Tman will be in position at Battery H.Q. under Bty Sm to act as carrying party if required.

                                                        [PTO]

8. The carrying party will take to each gun by 10.30 pm sufficient water to soak the sandbags on guns

9. Watches will be synchronised by 2/Lts GREAVES and DICKSON at Bde HQ ROUSEL at 5 pm 3rd May.

Zero will be at 11.30 pm 3rd May

10. Reports to Battery HQ
11. Acknowledge.

Issued at 2pm by D.R.

Copy 1 to 178 Inf Bde
    2 - 2/Lt Boys
    3 - 2/Lt Greaves
    4 - 2/Lt Dickson
    5&6 War Diary

R.A. Pratt Capt
OC 178 LTMB

East of HARGICOURT, from Aerial Photographs and O.Ps.

Scale 1:10000  Ref Sheets 62c N.E. & 62d N.W.

War Diary
of
178 Light Trench Mortar Battery
for month of June 1917

Vol ii

# WAR DIARY
## INTELLIGENCE SUMMARY
*(Erase heading not required.)*

Army Form C. 2118.

Instructions regarding War Diaries and Intelligence Summaries are contained in F.S. Regs., Part II. and the Staff Manual respectively. Title pages will be prepared in manuscript.

## 178 Light Trench Mortar Battery
### June 1917

| Hour, Date, Place | Summary of Events and Information | Remarks and references to Appendices |
|---|---|---|
| EQUANCOURT 1/6/17 6am | Proceeded by march route to METZ-EN-COUTURE | RM |
| METZ-EN-COUTURE 1/6/17 10pm | Took over from 126 Light T.M.B. the line from Q.12. a.6.7 to Q.5 d.2.7 with two guns at Q.11.a.2.7 and Headquarters and rest-billets in METZ-EN-COUTURE. | RM |
| METZ 1/6/17 to 11/6/17 | Battery engaged on R.E. work in HAVRINCOURT Wood and construction of dug-out at Q.5.d.0.1., also defensive gun emplacements at Q.11.C.2.8. and Q.5.C.5.3. | RM |
| METZ-EN-COUTURE 14/6/17 1pm | Battery relieved by 176 Light T.M.B. and proceeded to Brigade reserve in Camp at EQUANCOURT. | RM |
| EQUANCOURT 22/6/17 5am | Battery proceeded to IV Army School of Mortars for Battery Course of Instruction at VAUX-EN-AMIENOIS | RM |

Eachract from London Gazette —
2/Lt C.D.B. Boys to be acting Lieut while 2nd in command R.M.P of 178 Trench Mortar Battery 26 February 1917

R.A. Peaton Capt.
O.C. 178 Light T.M.B.

178th Light Trench Mortar Battery.

July 6 December 1916

Confidential

War Diary
178 Light Trench Mortar Battery
for month of
July 1917

Vol II

Army Form C. 2118.

# WAR DIARY
## or
## INTELLIGENCE SUMMARY.
(Erase heading not required.)

Instructions regarding War Diaries and Intelligence Summaries are contained in F. S. Regs., Part II. and the Staff Manual respectively. Title pages will be prepared in manuscript.

| Hour, Date, Place | Summary of Events and Information | Remarks and references to Appendices |
|---|---|---|
| | 178 Light Trench Mortar Battery | |
| | July 1917. | |
| 6am 3/7/17 Vaux-en-Amienois | Battery left to Army school of Instruction on completion of Course of Instruction and marched to Amiens for entrainment to rejoin the 178th Infantry Brigade. | Ref |
| 6pm 3/7/17 Peronne | Arrived at Peronne and remained for night at 39th Div Reinforcement camp | Ref |
| 2pm 4/7/17 Peronne | Entrained for Fins and from there marched to camp in Dessart Wood. | Ref |
| 4 Am 5/7/17 Line | Lieut C.D.B. Boys and N° 302409 Pte Birds G.H. wounded by hostile TM fire. | Ref |
| 11pm 5/7/17 Line | Relieved a section of the 177th T.M.B. with two guns in position at R7b 50.30 and R7b 4 5.30. | Ref |
| Night of 6/7 | Placed two guns in position, one at R7b 20.50 and one at R7a 90.50. | Ref |
| do — 11pm | Carried out punishment fire on "Thrush Trench" R7d 70.10 to R7d 10.60 in reply to hostile TM fire. | Ref |

# WAR DIARY
## or
## INTELLIGENCE SUMMARY.
*(Erase heading not required.)*

Army Form C. 2118.

Instructions regarding War Diaries and Intelligence Summaries are contained in F. S. Regs., Part II. and the Staff Manual respectively. Title pages will be prepared in manuscript.

| Hour, Date, Place | Summary of Events and Information | Remarks and references to Appendices |
|---|---|---|
| 7.30p 2/7/17 Line | Registered 4 guns on Plush Trench between R.1d.7 & and R.1d.1.b. | RAP |
| 10 pm — do — | Punishment fire on Plush Trench in reply to hostile T.M. fire | RAP |
| 6 pm 8/7/17 Line | Fired on Plush Trench in reply & grenatenwerfer fire | RAP |
| 6.30 pm — do — | Searched ground in front of Plush Trench for hostile snipers. | RAP |
| 2 am 9/7/17 | Relieved by the 174 L.T.M.B. and proceeded to Dessart Wood | RAP |
| 9 am 9/7/17 Dessart Wood | Proceeded by march route to Army Reserve encamp at O.35.d.5.b. (Sheet 57CSW) for training and rest. | RAP |
| 9am 13/7/17 O.35.d.5.b. | 2nd Lieut G.S.W. Profitt 2/8 B" Notts - Derby Regt attached for duty | RAP |

[Stamp: LIGHT TRENCH MORTAR BATTERY. 178TH INFANTRY BDE.]

R.A. Pratt Capt.
COMMDG. 178 BDE. TRENCH MORTAR BATT.

Confidential

War Diary
of
178 Light Trench Mortar Battery
for month of
August 1917.

Vol II

# WAR DIARY
## or
## INTELLIGENCE SUMMARY.

*(Erase heading not required.)*

Army Form C. 2118.

Sheet 1.

**178 Light Trench Mortar Battery 59th Div T.F.**

**August 1917**

| Hour, Date, Place | | Summary of Events and Information | Remarks and references to Appendices |
|---|---|---|---|
| 1-8-17 | Camp in OSSD | Battery still in Camp at OSSD Sheet 57c S.W. for general training | R.M. |
| 3/8/17 | - do - | Extract from G.H.Q. List of appointments No 46. Notts and Derby Rgt. 2nd Lieut H.P. Greaves to be actg Lt. whilst employed as 2nd in command 178 Light Trench Mortar Battery 6-7-17. Capt R.S. Pratt proceeded on 10 days leave to England. | R.M. |
| 5/8/17 | - do - | One other rank to 3rd Army Rest Camp. | R.M. |
| 6/8/17 | - do - | Two other ranks rejoined from IX Corps T.M. School BOVIES on completion of Instructors course | R.M. |
| 7/8/17 | - do - | Two other ranks visited III Army School of Sanitation at PERONNE. | R.M. |
| 9/8/17 | - do - | Two other ranks to Fenbries hospital | R.M. |
| 9/8/17 | - do - | 2nd Lieut G.S.W. Profit 7/8 Bn N.D. Rgt. taken on strength of Bn. Authority A.G. G.H.Q. No A/16119/254 c/9.8.17 | R.M. |
| 10/8/17 | - do - | Competition for detachments in clearing, firing and rapid coming into action won by No 3 and 4 detachments. Battery inspected by Brig General T.W. Stansfeld DSO and prizes for competition presented | R.M. |
| 11/8/17 | - do - | 2nd Lieut G.S.O. Profit to hospital with injury to shoulder | R.M. |

(9.29 6) W 3332-1107 100,000 10/13 HWV Forms/C. 2118/10.

Sheet 3

**Army Form C. 2118.**

# WAR DIARY
## or
## INTELLIGENCE SUMMARY.
*(Erase heading not required.)*

Instructions regarding War Diaries and Intelligence Summaries are contained in F.S. Regs. Part II. and the Staff Manual respectively. Title pages will be prepared in manuscript.

| Hour, Date, Place | | | Summary of Events and Information | Remarks and references to Appendices |
|---|---|---|---|---|
| | 13-8-17 | (Camp Oss?) | Capt R.S. Pratt rejoined from leave | R.H. |
| | 15-8-17 | - do - | Lieut H.P. Greaves proceeded on 10 days leave to England. One other rank to hospital sick | R.H. |
| | 18-8-17 | - do - | One other rank rejoined from sentry hospital | R.H. |
| | 19-8-17 | - do - | Two other ranks to III Army Rest Camp | R.H. |
| | 20-8-17 | - do - | One other rank rejoined from III Army Rest Camp. One other rank rejoined from IV Corps Gunnery School, ROVIES. From & from No 306825 L/Cpl Hinton HKG to paid Corporal, & 200989 Pte Woodruff T.W. to be paid L/Cpl. | R.H. |
| | 22-8-17 | - do - | One other rank from hospital | R.H. |
| | 23-8-17 | - do - | One other rank to hospital | R.H. |
| 8 am | 24-8-17 | - do - | Left for AVELUY. First half of journey by motor bus and second half by march route. | R.H. |
| 5 pm | | AVELUY | Arrived and went into camp in CAPSTAND HUTS nr W.10.c.93 Sheet 57D SE | R.H. |
| | 26-8-17 | - do - | One other rank from hospital | R.H. |
| 8 am | 28-8-17 | - do - | One other rank left as advance party for move to join V Army | R.H. |
| 12 noon | 29-8-17 | - do | 2nd Lieut F.A. Carlisle and one other rank reported for duty from 2/5th M.D. Regt. | R.H. |
| 10 pm 11.45 | - do - | - do - | Battery proceeded by march route to BEAUCOURT-SUR-ANCRE. R.H. and entrained. | R.H. |

Army Form C. 2118.

# WAR DIARY
## or
## INTELLIGENCE SUMMARY.
(Erase heading not required.)

| Hour, Date, Place | Summary of Events and Information | Remarks and references to Appendices |
|---|---|---|
| 1.30pm 31-8-17 Godwaersvelde | Detrained and proceeded by march route via STEENVOORDE and WINNEZEELE to billets on farm at J.1.a.2.9. Sheet 27. | Rpt. |

K. A. Platt
CAPT.
COMMDG. 178 BDE. TRENCH MORTAR BATT.

178th Inf Bde
Light T.M. Battery

WAR DIARY FOR SEPTEMBER 1917

Army Form C. 2118.

# WAR DIARY
## or
## INTELLIGENCE SUMMARY.
(Erase heading not required.)

Instructions regarding War Diaries and Intelligence Summaries are contained in F. S. Regs., Part II. and the Staff Manual respectively. Title pages will be prepared in manuscript.

178 Light Trench Mortar Battery, 59th Div T.F.

SEPTEMBER 1917

| Hour, Date, Place | Summary of Events and Information | Remarks and references to Appendices |
|---|---|---|
| 3.9.17 Farm J.1.a.29 (Sheet 27) | Capt. R.S. Root relinquished command of 178th LTMB to take up position as 2nd in Command of 2/6 Sh Staffords Brothers. | (HPL) |
| 4.9.17 do | Lieut H.P. Gregories assumed command of 178th Light T.M.B. acting Rank of Captain (GHQ Letter No 154) | |
| 4.9.17 do | 2nd Lt A.A. Dickson assumes 2nd in Command of 178th Light T.M.B. acting Rank of Lieut (GHQ Letter No 154) | |
| 4.9.17 do | 2nd Lt F.A. Myton (2/5 S.F.) 1 O.R. reports for duty. | |
| 3.pm 15.9.17 do | 2nd Battery Sports held. | |
| 15.9.17 do | Lieut A.A. Dickson proceeded to U.K. on 10 days leave. | |
| 9.9.17 do | No 307085 L/Cpl Bryslin H.B. promoted to Corporal. do | |
| 6.15am 20.9.17 do | Battery proceeded by Route march to WATOU district HQ. L.13.b.8.8. (Sheet 27) | |
| 4.pm 23.9.17 L.13.b.8.8 | do to BEDOUIN CAMP. HQ. G.6.d.3.9 (Sheet 28). | |
| 7.pm 24.9.17 BEDOUIN CAMP | 2 Officers, 8 NCO's & 34 O.R. proceed to WIELTJE (near YPRES) HQ. C.28.6.8.7 (Sheet 28) in readiness for attack at dawn on 26/9/17. Remainder of Battery stays behind at Transport lines | |
| 12.9.17 Farm J.1.a.9 | 2nd Lt F.A. Myton + 2 O.R. proceed on course at 19th Corps T.M. School. | |

Army Form C. 2118.

# WAR DIARY
or
# INTELLIGENCE SUMMARY.
(Erase heading not required.)

Instructions regarding War Diaries and Intelligence Summaries are contained in F.S. Regs., Part II. and the Staff Manual respectively. Title pages will be prepared in manuscript.

| Hour, Date, Place | | Summary of Events and Information | Remarks and references to Appendices |
|---|---|---|---|
| 25.9.17 | Jutlhus | Capt H.P Greaves reconnoitred position for 4 Stokes guns in + around SCHULLER GALLERIES (D.13. a.6.6. Sheet 29) | |
| 9 pm | do | 4 Guns moved into positions at SCHULLER GALLERIES. Ammunition convoys 1000 yds of positions by pack mules | |
| 5.50 am 26.9.17 | SCHULLER GALLERIES | Nos 2, 3, 5 & 8 guns under Capt H.P Greaves & 2nd Lt. E.A Carlisle fires 5 minute barrage onto CROSS COTTAGES, KANSAS HOUSE, GREEN HOUSE + neighbourhood, in conjunction with artillery barrage. 2nd Lt E.A. CARLISLE slightly wounded by shrapnel again wounded by shrapnel + evacuated. | |
| 6 am | do | do | |
| 7 pm | do | | |
| 11 am 27.9.17 | do | 4 guns, less 1 knapsack destroyed by hostile shell fire, withdrawn to WIELTJE. | |
| 27.9.17. | | Lieut A.A. Dickson returned from leave to UK + proceeded to take command of 125th L.T.M.B. | |
| 4.30 pm 29.9.17 | ST. JEAN. | Battery proceded from WIELTJE to No 2 area VLAMERTINGHE, suffering 30 casualties en route from hostile bombing | |
| 7 pm 29.9.17 | VLAMERTINGHE | Battery arrived in rest billets HQ. H.Q. C.7.7. (Sheet 28). | |
| 10 pm 27.9.17 | do | 2nd Lt. E.A. Myton + 2 O.R. arrives back from Course at 19th Corps T-M School | |

H.P Greaves
M.P. Capt T.M.B.
O/C 178th Light T.M.B

WAR DIARY
FOR
OCTOBER/1917

178th Light Trench Mortar Battery.

Army Form C. 2118.

# WAR DIARY
## INTELLIGENCE SUMMARY.
*(Erase heading not required.)*

Instructions regarding War Diaries and Intelligence Summaries are contained in F. S. Regs., Part II. and the Staff Manual respectively. Title pages will be prepared in manuscript.

| Hour, Date, Place | | | Summary of Events and Information | Remarks and references to Appendices |
|---|---|---|---|---|
| | | | **178th Light Trench Mortar Battery – 59th Div T.F.** | |
| | | | **OCTOBER 1917** | |
| 9-30 pm | 1/10/17 | VLAMERTINGHE | Battery entrained and proceeded to STEENBECK by rail, thence by route march to WITTES. HQ at farm on WITTES- CALAIS ROAD. (Sheet HAZEBROUCK 5A) | |
| 3.0 pm | 4/10/17 | BOESEGHEM | Battery reviewed by Divisional General. | |
| 8.0 am | 6/10/17 | WITTES | Battery proceeded partly by route march & partly by bus to billets in COYECQUE (Sheet HAZEBROUCK 5A) Billet No 20 (opposite COYECQUE church). | |
| 6.0 pm | 6/10/17 | COYECQUE | Reinforcement arrived, 17 O.R. | |
| 6.0 pm | 9/10/17 | do | Lieut J.P. MAINE +1 O.R. reported for duty. | |
| 9.0 am | 10/10/17 | do | Battery proceeded by Route March to SACHIN where it was billeted for the night. (Sheet LENS II). | |
| 9.0 am | 11/10/17 | SACHIN | Battery proceeded by Route March to CAMBLAIN CHATELAIN & billeted for the night (Sheet LENS II) | |
| 11.0 am | 12/10/17 | CAMBLAIN CHATELAIN | Battery proceeded by Route March to BARLIN & billeted for the night (Sheet LENS II) HQ at ESTAMINET HOLLAIN BARRE. | |
| 9.30 am | 13/10/17 | BARLIN | Battery proceeded by Route March to PETIT SERVINS to test billets & men & stores enfint No16 HQ at Billet No 31 map ry SHEET 36B. Q.35.a.2.8 | |
| 6.0 pm | 16/10/17 | PETIT SERVINS | 8 O.R. arrived as reinforcements | |
| 9.0 am | 17/10/17 | do | 2nd Lieut H.N SHAW (3/6SF) +1 O.R. reported for duty | |
| 11.0 am | 18/10/17 | do | Lieut J.P. MAINE admitted to Hospital - Sick. | |

Army Form C. 2118.

# WAR DIARY
## or
## INTELLIGENCE SUMMARY.
*(Erase heading not required.)*

Instructions regarding War Diaries and Intelligence Summaries are contained in F.S. Regs., Part II. and the Staff Manual respectively. Title pages will be prepared in manuscript.

| Hour, Date, Place | Summary of Events and Information | Remarks and references to Appendices |
|---|---|---|
| 18.10.17. PETIT SERVINS. | CAPT H.P. GREAVES & 2nd LIEUT W.E. MYTON reconnoitred the AVION sector of the line (S. of LENS) | |
| 20.10.17 do | 2nd LIEUT H.N. SHAW do do do do | |
| Night of 21/22nd/10/17 | Relieved the 114th/Light TMB in the line taking over 6 guns in the AVION Sector (LENS). Battery HQ at cellar in brewery LA COULOTTE, N31.c.3.0 (Sheet 36c). HQ to the line in cellar of house in AVION at N32.B.50.25 (Sheet 36c). 2nd Lt W.E Myton took first duty in the line there being 5 effective guns as follows. 2 in positions at N32.b.50.25, 1 at N32.d.65.65, 2 in CYRIL TRENCH at 73.a.80.80, 73.a.75.80 (Sheet 36c) | |
| 23.10.17 In the Line | Nos 4 + 5 emplacements adapted for offensive work and registered on SALINE TRENCH (N33a) & enemy T.M. positions behind Railway in N33.a. | (N32.65.25) |
| 25.10.17 In the Line. | No 3 Emplacement (N32.d.65.65) adapted for offensive work & registered on E & SE part of SLAG HEAP in N33.a. | |
| Night of 25/26-10-17 do | 2nd Lieut H.N. Shaw & half battery relieved 2nd Lt H.N Myton & half battery in the line. | |
| Night of 29/30-10-17 do | 2nd/Lieut W.E Myton & half battery relieved 2nd Lt H.N Shaw & ½ battery | |
| 30.10.17 do | The positions in CYRIL TR continued & 2 guns withdrawn. | |
| 30.10.17 do | New position constructed at QUEBEC RD N32.d.90.80 and a gun placed there. | |

Army Form C. 2118.

# WAR DIARY
## or
## INTELLIGENCE SUMMARY.
*(Erase heading not required.)*

Instructions regarding War Diaries and Intelligence Summaries are contained in F. S. Regs., Part II. and the Staff Manual respectively. Title pages will be prepared in manuscript.

| Hour, Date, Place | Summary of Events and Information | Remarks and references to Appendices |
|---|---|---|
| 23/10/17 to 31/10/17 In the Line | During these 8 days the following targets were engaged. <br><br> Hostile T.M. positions behind Railway in N33a. <br> SALINE trench } <br> SALLY do } and Junction in N33a. <br> Hostile positions in vicinity of SLAG HEAP in N33c+d <br> Hostile mobile M.G in Copse N27c <br><br> Approximately 360 rounds of Stokes Shells were fired at ranges varying from 550 to 750 yds. | Ref Sheet 36c + LENS |

JF Greaves
2/Lt Capt. 7 M/S
Cdg "175" Light [?]

178th Light T.M.B

WAR DIARY

NOVEMBER
1917

Army Form C. 2118.

# WAR DIARY
## ~~INTELLIGENCE SUMMARY~~
*(Erase heading not required.)*

Instructions regarding War Diaries and Intelligence Summaries are contained in F.S. Regs., Part II. and the Staff Manual respectively. Title pages will be prepared in manuscript.

| Hour, Date, Place | Summary of Events and Information | Remarks and references to Appendices |
|---|---|---|
| | **178th/ light Trench Mortar Battery. — 59th Div" T.F.** | |
| | **NOVEMBER 1917.** | |
| November 1st – 6th/11/17. In Line. AVION SECTOR. | During these 6 days, normal retaliatory targets were engaged, 200 rounds being fired. | |
| 8 pm 6/7 Nov. 17. do | Battery relieved by 176th T.M.B & proceeded to rest billets at GOUY SERVINS. (Map Sheet 36 B). | |
| 11 am. 14/11/17. GOUY-SERVINS | Battery proceeded by march route to "Y" HUTS, ETRUN | |
| 5 pm 19/11/17 ETRUN. | Battery proceeded by march route to HENDECOURT-LES-RANSART. | |
| 9-0 pm 20/11/17. HENDECOURT. | do do do to GOMIECOURT. | |
| 1-30 pm 23/11/17 GOMIECOURT | do do do to BIHUCOURT WEST and entrained there to FINS, marching from FINS TO EQUANCOURT. | |
| 1-15 pm 29/11/17. EQUANCOURT | Battery proceeded by march route to RIBECOURT, thence back to dugouts in old BRITISH FRONT LINE at TRESCAULT (map 57c) | |

N. Sheaves Capt.

**WAR DIARY**
or
**INTELLIGENCE SUMMARY.**

Army Form C. 2118.

178 TMB

| Hour, Date, Place | | Summary of Events and Information | Remarks and references to Appendices |
|---|---|---|---|
| Dec 1-3/17 | TRESCAULT | In old British front line at TRESCAULT. | |
| 4 pm 3/12/17 | FLESQUIERES | Battery proceeded by motor lorry via RIBECOURT to FLESQUIERES and relieved 176 TMB in the line. Battery HQ in dugout in sunken road at L19 a.1.9. New gun places in defensive positions at L13 c.15.30 + L13 c.40.30. | Reports 57 C |
| 4/12/17 | do. | Alternative teams emplacement constructed at K24 c.95.60, K24 B.90.80, L19 a.10.30. 4 guns manned in all. | do |
| 3 pm 6/12/17 | do | Enemy attacked from direction of BOURLON WOOD & ANNEUX — Battery fired 50 rounds. Later parties of enemy came in range. Good results obtained. | do |
| 5 pm 7/12/17 | do. | Battery relieved in right sector of FLESQUIERES front by 177 TMB. — Proceeded to take over 2 positions in left sector at K17 d.90.50. Battery HQ moved to dugout in sunken road at K24 d.50.80 | |
| 6 pm 8/12/17 | do | 3 men killed in endeavouring to construct new positions at K18 c.10.80. H Q dugout in left sector at K18 c.10.60 blown in — 1 man wounded | |
| 6 pm 9/12/17 | do | Battery relieved 177 TMB in right sector. Took over T.M. defences of both sectors. Two new positions constructed at K18 c.60.50. 2 guns in each place also | |

# WAR DIARY
## or
## INTELLIGENCE SUMMARY.
*(Erase heading not required.)*

Army Form C. 2118.

Instructions regarding War Diaries and Intelligence Summaries are contained in F. S. Regs., Part II. and the Staff Manual respectively. Title pages will be prepared in manuscript.

| Hour, Date, Place | Summary of Events and Information | Remarks and references to Appendices |
|---|---|---|
| 10/12/17 - FLESQUIERES | Revised location of guns as follows: <br> @ LEFT SECTOR { 2 guns at K18 c.16.5 50 <br> @ RIGHT do { 3 guns at L13 c.10.30 <br> L13 c.25.30 <br> L19 a.65.65. | Ref 57C. |
| 12/12/17 do | 2 offensive posts's constructed at L13c.30.55. | do |
| 5 am 13/12/17 do. | Enemy Gunpits & area at L13a were engaged by our mortars - 30 rounds fired | do |
| 11 pm 14/12/17 do | Carried out pre-arranged bombardment of enemy strong points & posts in connection with raid by our infantry - 100 rounds fired. | do |
| 5.0 pm 15/12/17 do | Fired 12 rounds onto enemy MG position at L13 d.50.95. | do |
| 9.0 pm 16/12/17 do | Relieved in both sectors by 177 T.M.B. - Battery proceeds to dugouts in sunken road at K29 d.10.40 | do |
| 12.0 noon 18/12/17 | Battery proceeds by route march via HAVRINCOURT BERTINCOURT | do |
| 2.0 pm 20/12/19 BERTINCOURT | do do to BARASTRE. | do |

Army Form C. 2118.

# WAR DIARY
## or
## INTELLIGENCE SUMMARY.
*(Erase heading not required.)*

Instructions regarding War Diaries and Intelligence Summaries are contained in F. S. Regs., Part II. and the Staff Manual respectively. Title pages will be prepared in manuscript.

| Hour, Date, Place | Summary of Events and Information | Remarks and references to Appendices |
|---|---|---|
| 1.30pm 23.12.17 BARASTRE | Battery proceeded by march route to BEAULENCOURT | Ref 57c |
| 7.0am 25.12.17 BEAULENCOURT | Battery proceeded by march route to BARAUME, thence by train (via ACHIET LE GRAND-MAROEUIL-TINQUES-ST POL) and march route to MONCHIEAUX. | Ref 57c & 51c. |

A.E. Naylor 2 Lieut.
O/c 178 Light Trench Mortar Battery.

(9 29 6) W 3332—1107 100,000 10/13 H W V Forms/C. 2118/10.

178th Light T.M.B.

WAR DIARY - JANUARY
1918.

Army Form C. 2118.

# WAR DIARY
## or
## INTELLIGENCE SUMMARY.
*(Erase heading not required.)*

Instructions regarding War Diaries and Intelligence Summaries are contained in F. S. Regs., Part II. and the Staff Manual respectively. Title pages will be prepared in manuscript.

| Hour, Date, Place | Summary of Events and Information | Remarks and references to Appendices |
|---|---|---|
| | 178th LIGHT TRENCH MORTAR BATTERY — JANUARY 1918. | |
| MONCHEAUX — 8/1/18. | Brigade Cross Country Races — won by 178th T.M.B. | Map Ref 51c. |
| AMBINES — 19/1/18 | Battery fired a practice live shoot of 40 rounds on range at VI Corps T.M. School. | do. |
| MONCHEAUX — 28/1/18. | Stokes Gun Competition. — 1st Prize awarded to No 8 Detachment (A/Cpl Thursby) — 2nd Prize awarded to No 4 Detachment (Cpl Buckland). | do |
| do. 26/1/18 | 2nd Lt Hallworth M.O.R. reports for duty. | do |
| do 30/1/18. | G.O.C. Brigade presents Stokes Gun Competition Prizes + inspects the Battery. | do |

F. J. Greaves
CAPT.
CDG. 178th LIGHT TRENCH MORTAR BATTERY.

# WAR DIARY
## for
## FEBRUARY 1918

178th Light Trench Mortar Battery.

# WAR DIARY
## INTELLIGENCE SUMMARY.
*(Erase heading not required.)*

Army Form C. 2118.

| Hour, Date, Place | Summary of Events and Information | Remarks and references to Appendices |
|---|---|---|
| | 178th LIGHT T.M.B. — FEBRUARY 1918. | |
| | 3rd Battery Sports held | Ref Sheet 51c |
| 2.0pm. 1/2/18 MONCHEAUX | | |
| 9.30am. 8/2/18 do | Battery proceeded by march route to BARLY, via GRAND - RULLECOURT - Billeted for the night. | 51c |
| 10.0am. 9/2/18 BARLY | Battery proceeded by march route to "B" LINES, DURHAM CAMP, BOISLEUX ST MARC. | do 51c + 51B |
| 10.0am 10/2/18 BOISLEUX ST MARC | Battery proceeded by march route to NORTH CAMP, MORY. | do 51B |
| 9.45am to 3.0pm 11/2/18 MORY. | Battery relieved the 119th LIGHT T.M.B. in the line, in the LEFT Sector of the DIVISIONAL FRONT, N. of BULLECOURT, taking over. 5 Defensive Emplacements at U.20.B. 45.26 U.20.B. 25.85 U.20.a.80.80. U.20.a.80.90. U.14.0.40.40. Battery HQ in Sunken rd at U.25.d.80.20. Line HQ in dugout in QUEEN'S LANE at U.20.a.50.30. Left Section under 2nd A. Harris in the line. Right Section in reserve at Battery HQ. | do 51B. |
| 14/2/18 In the Line. | New Offensive emplacement constructed at U.21.a.60.10. - called "A" PIT. | do 51b Trench map. |

Army Form C. 2118.

# WAR DIARY
## or
## INTELLIGENCE SUMMARY.
(Erase heading not required.)

Instructions regarding War Diaries and Intelligence Summaries are contained in F. S. Regs., Part II. and the Staff Manual respectively. Title pages will be prepared in manuscript.

| Hour, Date, Place | Summary of Events and Information | Remarks and references to Appendices |
|---|---|---|
| Whaline, Midnight, 14/2/18. | 16 rounds fired by No 1 Gun from "A" PIT onto DOG TRENCH & TRIDENT ALLEY (U 21 b) | Ref Sheet 51 b. |
| do. 2 am & 5 am 17/2/18 | 23 rounds fired by No 2. Gun onto VULCAN ALLEY in U 15 c. New pit for No 1. Gun completed at U 20 b 50.15 | do. |
| do 8 pm 15/2/18 | Right Section, under 2nd Lt T.L. HILL relieved the Left Section. | do |
| do 8 pm 18/2/18 | 24 rds fired onto JUNCTION of DOG TRENCH & TRIDENT ALLEY | do |
| do 9 pm 20/2/18 | Left Section, under 2nd Lt A.Chrins relieved Right Section in the Zone. | do |
| do 1 am 22/2/18 | 20 rds fired by No 1. Gun on DOG TRENCH & TRIDENT ALLEY 20 " " No 2. do " VULCAN ALLEY. | do |
| do 22/2/18 | New Offensive Pit, Arc "B" PIT, completed at U14 c 95.65 | do |
| do Midnight 23/2/18 | 40 rds fired onto MATCH ALLEY, COPSE TRENCH & VULCAN ALLEY. | do |
| do 2.30 & 4 am 25/2/18 | 30 rds fired onto MATCH ALLEY & CRUMP ALLEY | do |
| do 24/2/18 | Concrete Pill Box used by No 2. Gun crew received direct hit from enemy shell – no one injured. | do. |
| do 9.30 pm 25/2/18 | 34 rds fired onto VULCAN ALLEY & SUNKEN RD in U 15 c & U 14 d in response to S.O.S | do |
| do 10.30 pm 26/2/18 | 10 rds fired on to MATCH ALLEY in U 15 a. | do |

Ref Trench Map.

[signature]
CAPT.
O.C. 178TH LIGHT TRENCH MORTAR BATTERY.

178 L.T.M. Bty
(59 Divn)

# WAR DIARY
## INTELLIGENCE SUMMARY
*(Erase heading not required.)*

Army Form C. 2118.

Instructions regarding War Diaries and Intelligence Summaries are contained in F.S. Regs., Part II. and the Staff Manual respectively. Title pages will be prepared in manuscript.

| Hour, Date, Place | Summary of Events and Information | Remarks and references to Appendices |
|---|---|---|
| 2.3.18. In the line. | Battery retained in the line by the 102nd Light T.M. Battery. Battery proceeded to MORY by march route via CROISILLES & ST LEGER. | Ref Map 51 B |
| 12 Noon 10.3.18. MORY | Battery proceeded by march route to CGD 46 and thence to 102nd Light T.M. Battery taking over ground B5b2N, B6b3.4, B4b8.4, B.4.8.5, B5 6Q9, B5.6.10. also C.10.b.6.6. | Ref Map 51 B SW. |
| 21.3.18. In the line. | Enemy attacked about 9.50a.m. after four and a half hours artillery bombardment. Battery fired 3 Officers (2 missing, 1 wounded missing) + 56 rank + file sent Infm. gun. etc. | Ref Map LENS 11. |
| 22.3.18. AYETTE | Battery retreated to 2/5th Bn. Sherwood Foresters. Bttry moved from ERNILLERS to AYETTE | do |
| 23.3.18. 7.0am. AYETTE | Battery moved by march route with 2/5 Bn. Sherwood Foresters to SENLIS. | Sheet AMIENS 19. |
| 25.3.18. 2.30am. SENLIS | Battery moved by march route with 2/5 Bn. Sherwood Foresters to BAVELINCOURT. | Sheet LENS 11. |
| 26.3.18. 4.30am. BAVELINCOURT | Battery moved by march route with 2/5 Bn. Sherwood Foresters to FIEFFES. | Sheet LENS 11. |
| 28.3.18. 10.10am. FIEFFES | Battery proceeded with 2/5 Bn. Sherwood Foresters by march route to CANDAS, entrained to LAPUGNOY, by lorries to GAMBLIGNEUL. | |

W.C. Taylor Lieut.
Cdg 1/8th Light T.renel Mortar Battery.

From O.C.
    178th Light T.M.Battery.

To 178th Inf.Bde.
-------------------------

Ref. Sheets 51b S.W. &  Sheet 57c N.W.

Sir,

On the 21st inst. I was at battle headquarters in a dug-out on the sunken road at C.9.d.7.7. with Capt. H.P.Greaves.

At about 5.0 a.m. we were awakened by heavy enemy gunfire, which before we finished dressing had extended to the sunken road.

In an hour's time all the Machine Gun Company's wires to the front were cut. Up to then the only messages received had been that they were alright, I understood this to refer to the signallers at the other end.

At 9.30 a.m. no information was obtainable. Capt. Greaves went to the 5th Bn. H.Q. but could get none. On returning he sent two men forward to get to our Left Section H.Q. in RAILWAY RESERVE at C.5.a.1.5. Sheet 57c N.W. These men never returned.

About 10.30 a.m. 2/Lt. T.L.Hill came back. He was wounded in the right foot. He reported that the Hun was in the front line and GOOLE ALLEY. The two trench-mortars we had mounted, the latter were blown up before the S.O.S. went up. The teams left GOOLE ALLEY with the infantry and withdrew to RAILWAY RESERVE where 2/Lieut. Hill was wounded.

Captain Greaves ordered battery headquarters to stand to. The spare reserve gun was got out and mounted about C.9.d.9.5. Sheet 57c N.W.

After this I have no idea of time, and men in the road, I estimated the number at about 200 were got into firing positions on the front edge of the road and were very cool except for the first low-flying aeroplane. When this came over some few made a rush for cover but were got back and there was no further trouble. At this time the enemy barrage appeared to be on the road in C.10.a. & c. Sheet 57c N.W. Soon after it lifted on to us, I did not see any signal at all just before it lifted. It was heavy but did not get fairly on the road most of it was behind. I should estimate that it rested there twenty minutes.

When the barrage lifted I saw the Bosche in the valley in C.10.c. (57c S.W.) and heard man saying he was bombing the trenches in front but this I could not see. We commenced firing the gun on to area round C.10 central (57c N.W.).

For some time the situation remained like this, a few men tried to come over the top but were easily dispersed and the enemy seemed to be held, then they were seen on the road about C.9.b.5.0. (57c N.W.) but these were shot or retired. Then they started bombing up SYDNEY AVENUE but Major Trench started counter-bombing and stopped them for a time. Soon after Major Trench was killed near the top of the 2/5th Bn H.Q. dug-out and my runner was shot in the back from the rear. Then Capt. Greaves came and told me to get some more ammunition down for the gun, but just then I saw Huns advancing up to us from NOREUIL village and said "We had better make a defensive flank in NOREUIL Switch". He agreed and said "See to it", so I took two of the battery men as runners and about 20 of the 2/5th men and a Lewis gun into this trench, and they got into action against them. I then found that men of the 177th Inf.Bde. were in the trench, but apparently unaware of the enemy's nearness, so I went to inform them. On turning round to return I found the Bosche between me and the men I had left, and then he started sweeping the trench with machine guns, as far as I could gather from somewhere about the far edge of NOREUIL.

I then went back along the trench showing all the 177th Bde officers and N.C.Os where the enemy were, and helping to get the men to the proper places. I found a party in one place firing across the opposite way, and from there saw enemy troops on the ridge in C.9.c. (57c N.W.).   No-one retired from the sunken road between the western end of SYDNEY AVENUE and NOREUIL for I should have seen them.

When all the 177th Inf.Bde. people were all right, I did not know what further to do, and decided to report what I knew to Brigade H.Q., and set out the ground around where the Decauville track splits, one line to MORY and the other towards the Dressing Station in the valley in front of VRAUCOURT was swept by several machine guns from the direction of NOREUIL.

I reached Bde H.Q. and reported as you know.

Special points I noticed during the fighting were that hardly any wounded at all came back from the trenches in front. The only officers I saw were Capt. Wright of the 7th Bn Sher.Fors and one other officer of the same Bn whom I did not know.

Enemy low-flying aeroplanes came over and fired white Very lights, I could not make out whether these were contact signals or whether they were to show the enemy where we were.  I did not notice any difference in the shell fire after their visit, nor did I see any signals fired from the ground for them.

The enemy had their steel helmets covered with sand-bag material in many cases making them more difficult to identify in trenches.

The break-through guns in RAILWAY RESERVE C.5 central and C.4.d.9.7. did not fire as far as I can find out because no-one knew where our infantry were.   I have not been able to find out what happened to the guns at C.5 central, except that they did not fire.

I could not find anyone who had seen the S.O.S. signal go up.

27.3.18.

(Sd) W.E.Myton, Lieut.
O.C. 178 L.T.M.B.

Copy of letter from Captain H.P.Greaves (Commdg. 178th L.T.
Mortar Battery) to Br.-General T.W.Stansfield.

4 Gordon Street,
Burton-on-Trent.

5. 2. 19.

My dear General Stansfield,

    I was very pleased to receive your kind and interesting letter of the 2nd inst. and in accordance with your wish I am giving you below a brief and private a/c of the events (as I remember them) of the 21st.

<u>5 a.m.</u>  Myton and myself were awakened by the Boche barrage. I immediately gave the "alert". By 6 a.m. my dug-out was completely blown in at the entrance and it took us <u>over 2 hours</u> to dig ourselves out. Judd and Smith-Masters were both down my dug-out at this time. I then went on top - sent down 2 runners to Lieut. Harris (who was in Rly. Reserve) to get definite news as all telephone communication was cut. Our sunken road was very heavily shelled with 5.9's and gas shells. About 9.30 a.m. wounded started to arrive from the front, with garbled a/c's of what was happening. Later 2/Lieut. Hill was brought to my H.Q. badly wounded in the leg and foot. Of his two gun teams, several men had been killed - one gun destroyed by direct hit, and the other he blew up himself. 3 of Harris's guns in Rly. Reserve did some good shooting. When it became evident that "Rly. Reserve" had "gone under", I offered myself, Myton, and some 12 men to Col. Gadd, and of course he accepted us, and put Major Trench and myself in charge of the Sunken road. Shortly after, Trench was killed, only a few yards away from me, in gallantly leading a bombing raid. I immediately reported this fact to Col. Gadd and also told him our flanks were being encircled rapidly. I them tried to carry on in the Sunken Rd, and managed to organize a few firing bays, and for a time we kept the Boche off, although he still crept round our flanks (he came in crowds down the Noreuil Valley). I was then hit in the left thigh by a lump of shrapnel but as it was not very serious I kept on and brought the one Stokes gun I had with me at H.Q. into action. Meanwhile I told Myton to take ½ dozen men (it was all I could spare) and try and guard my right flank (Noreuil Valley). <u>That was the last I saw of Myton and he certainly received no orders from me to go back.</u> Previous to this, thinking we were in for a "thick time" I ordered L/Cpl. Fretwell to take my Stationery box and papers to Bde. H.Q. and report there. I believe he got through alright.

The Boche then started to enfilade the Sunken Rd. with a machine gun from my right. I managed to knock out this M.G. with our last Stokes gun, but lost several men in doing so. By this time our numbers were getting thin, and I deemed it advisable to again acquaint Col. Gadd of the situation, which was then desperate. I therefore went down his dug-out and reported to him and he told me to try and get the men back to the next defence system. I went on top again, and managed to get a few men back. The Boche was rapidly encircling us. He again enfiladed our Sunken Rd. with machine guns, and unfortunately I ran out of Stokes shells, so we destroyed the gun. A few minutes later I was hit by a m.g. bullet through the head, and when the Boche got me I was unconcious (or thereabouts).

I believe Judd (padre) was killed, and Smith-Masters was taken prisoner. Both my subalterns, Hill and Harris, were wounded and taken prisoner. I cannot speak too highly of the courage and coolness displayed by Major Trench.

...............................

I am, Sir,

Yours very sincerely,

(sgd) H.P.Greaves.

(Capt. Commdg. 178th L.T.Mortar Batt)

Army Form C. 2118.

# WAR DIARY
## or
## INTELLIGENCE SUMMARY.
(Erase heading not required.)

Instructions regarding War Diaries and Intelligence Summaries are contained in F.S. Regs., Part II. and the Staff Manual respectively. Title pages will be prepared in manuscript.

| Hour, Date, Place | Summary of Events and Information | Remarks and references to Appendices |
|---|---|---|
| APRIL 1st CAMBLIGNEUL | MARCHED TO AUBIGNY WHERE BATTY entrained. Detrained at PROVEN and marched to ST JEAN-TER-BEIZEN. | |
| APR 2nd | Training and reorganisation. | |
| " 3rd | Inspection by Gen PLUMER Comdg 2nd Army | |
| " 4 to 6th | Training | |
| " 7 | Battery moved by march route to WINNEZEELE Billeted in Orchard | Sheet 27 U17&5 6 |
| " 8 & 9th | Training | |
| " 10th | Battery moved by train & march route to BRANDHOEK and into hole camp 15. | Sheet 28 H8 C 8 6 |
| " 11th | Training. Lieut T Hornall took over command of Battery | |
| " 12 | Battery moved by light Rly & Railway march route to BRANDOUTRE and on the last 1/4 park Sheet 28 N14 & | |
| " 13 to 18th | Battery ached to 4 Yo A.A/60 R.A. for working parties dug posts on foot of Kennel Hill | |
| 19th | Moved to WESTOUTRE area | Casualties 3 killed and 3 wounded |
| " 20th | Moved by Light Rly & march route to POPERINGHE area in huts & Private Camp. | Map of Sheet 28 A 30 d.1.3 |
| " 21st | Moved by march route to HOUTKERQUE for camp | Sheet 27 F 2 6 central |
| " 22nd 23 | Training | Sheet 27 L 30 1 4 |
| " 24 | Moved by march route to JAN TER BEIZEN in huts & Private Camp | |
| " 25 | Training | |
| " 26 27 28 | Moved by march route to HOUTKERQUE for camp | Map of Sheet 27 L 20 central |
| " 29 | | |
| " 30 | Training | |

H Hornall Lieut.

Cmdg 178 Light Trench Morter

Army Form C. 2118.

# WAR DIARY
## *or*
## INTELLIGENCE SUMMARY.
*(Erase heading not required.)*

Instructions regarding War Diaries and Intelligence Summaries are contained in F.S. Regs., Part II. and the Staff Manual respectively. Title pages will be prepared in manuscript.

| Hour, Date, Place | Summary of Events and Information | Remarks and references to Appendices |
|---|---|---|
| 9.45am 5.5.18. HOUTKERQUE | Battery moved to ST OMER by employees | Sheet 2 R. |
| 7.5.18. ST OMER | Battery temporarily disbanded. Personnel despatched to base | |

W. Whyte Kirk.
for O.C. 178 S.S.M.B.

Army Form C. 2118.

# WAR DIARY
# INTELLIGENCE SUMMARY.
(Erase heading not required.)

Instructions regarding War Diaries and Intelligence Summaries are contained in F. S. Regs., Part II. and the Staff Manual respectively. Title pages will be prepared in manuscript.

| Place | Date | Hour | Summary of Events and Information | Remarks and references to Appendices |
|---|---|---|---|---|
| | | | CONFIDENTIAL

WAR DIARY OF 178TH L.T.M. BATTERY.

From 1st June 1918 to 30th June 1918

VOLUME 1 | |

Army Form C. 2118.

# WAR DIARY
## or
## INTELLIGENCE SUMMARY.

178th Light Trench Mortar Battery

(Erase heading not required.)

Instructions regarding War Diaries and Intelligence Summaries are contained in F. S. Regs., Part II. and the Staff Manual respectively. Title pages will be prepared in manuscript.

| Place | Date | Hour | Summary of Events and Information | Remarks and references to Appendices |
|---|---|---|---|---|
| FONTAINE LES BOULANS | 24/6/18 | | Battery formed under Command of Capt. A Barker M.C. with two officers and forty one other ranks from Batteries in the Brigade | AA |
| Hesdin - 30/6/18 | 24/6/18 - 30/6/18 | | Preliminary training carried out - Gun drill etc | AA |

Thornett Lieut.
O.C.

Army Form C. 2118.

# WAR DIARY
## or
## INTELLIGENCE SUMMARY.
(Erase heading not required.)

178th Light Trench Mortar Battery

VOLUME II

Instructions regarding War Diaries and Intelligence Summaries are contained in F. S. Regs., Part II. and the Staff Manual respectively. Title pages will be prepared in manuscript.

| Place | Date | Hour | Summary of Events and Information | Remarks and references to Appendices |
|---|---|---|---|---|
| FONTAINE-LES-BOULANS | 11/7/18 to 12/7/18 | | Battery training | J.P. |
| | 12/7/18 | | Lieut Tannett (Royal West Kent) took over command of Battery vice Capt Barber to Brigade H.Q. | |
| | 13/7/18 | | Battery training | |
| | 14/7/18 | | Battery attended Church Parade | |
| | 15th to 20/7/18 | | Battery training | |
| " | 21/7/18 | | Battery Inspect. Forty four other ranks taken on the strength. Twelve one other ranks attached to Battery from Battalion, to act as Carriers | J.P. |
| " | 21/7/18 | | Battery attended Church Parade | |
| " | 22/7/18 | | Battery training | |
| " | 23/7/18 to 26/7/18 | | Battery moved to Barly in lorries and billeted Pts A.8.7 Sheet 51 C SE | J.P. |
| BARLY | 27/7/18 | | Battery having including dummy firing | |
| " | 28/7/18 | | Battery attended Church Parade | |
| " | 29th to 3/8/18 | | Battery training | J.P. |

J. Harnett Lieut. O.C.

# CONFIDENTIAL

# WAR DIARY

## OF

## 178th Light Trench Mortar Battery

## AUGUST 1918.

Army Form C. 2118.

# WAR DIARY
or
## INTELLIGENCE SUMMARY.
(Erase heading not required.)

**178th Light Trench Mortar Battery**

**VOLUME II**

Instructions regarding War Diaries and Intelligence Summaries are contained in F.S. Regs., Part II. and the Staff Manual respectively. Title pages will be prepared in manuscript.

| Place | Date | Hour | Summary of Events and Information | Remarks and references to Appendices |
|---|---|---|---|---|
| BARLY | 1/8/18 | | Battery training | |
| " | 2/8/18 | 4:30 pm | Battery entrained (Light Railway) for the Line | |
| BLAIRVILLE | 2nd & 3rd midnight 3/8 | | Battery relieved 76th L.T.M.B. in the night Sector of Desvres front No 1 Section taking over forward guns – No 2 Section in reserve at Blairville Quarries | SHEET 51C.SE. R 34 D 3.3 |
| " | 4th to 7/8/18 | | Battery working on new emplacements in the line | |
| " | 8/8/18 | | No 2 Section under Lieut Stewart relieved No 1 Section under 2nd Lieut Lebaton | |
| " | 9th to 11/8/18 | | Work continued on S.O.S. Emplacements | |
| " | 12/8/18 | | S.O.S. Emplacements completed. Guns under Lieut Stewart brought back from forward positions to S.O.S. positions. | |
| " | 13th to 16/8/18 | | Battery working to improve Emplacements | |
| " | 17/8/18 | midnight | Battery relieved by the 177th L.T.M.B. on completion of relief. Battery moved to Barly area in Divisional Reserve | |
| BARLY | 18/8/18 | | Battery resting and cleaning up. | |
| " | 19/8/18 | | Battery training. | |

# WAR DIARY or INTELLIGENCE SUMMARY

Army Form C. 2118.

**VOLUME III**

178th Light Trench Mortar Battery

(Erase heading not required.)

Instructions regarding War Diaries and Intelligence Summaries are contained in F.S. Regs., Part II. and the Staff Manual respectively. Title pages will be prepared in manuscript.

| Place | Date | Hour | Summary of Events and Information | Remarks and references to Appendices |
|---|---|---|---|---|
| BARLY | 20/8/18 | | Battery to Bathe and training. | L/A |
| " | 21/8/18 | midnight | Battery entrained and moved to Blairville | |
| BLAIRVILLE | 21st/22nd 8/18 | " | Battery relieved 3rd Guards Brigade L.T.M.B. | |
| " | 22/8/18 | " | Guns and Teams withdrawn from line to Headquarters, Blairville | |
| " | 23/8/18 | | Battery moved by march route to Saulty | |
| SAULTY | 24/8/18 | | (Battery entrained for Tyler Army area – detraining at Berguette. Battery moved by march route to Ham-en-Artois being billetted O27D (10.35) | SHEET 36A 2/1- |
| HAM-EN-ARTOIS | 25th/26/8/18 | " | Battery training | |
| " | 27/8/18 | | Battery moved to St Venant being billetted in Asylum at P9 Central | SHEET 36A L/A |
| ST. VENANT | 28/8/18 | | Taking over duties of Support Brigade T.M.B. relieving the 177th L.T.M.B. | |
| " | 29/8/18 | | Battery training | |
| " | 30/8/18 | | Battery having 4 trucking new emplacements to cover front line of Support Brigade | |

J. Hearne H. Capt.

Confidential

War Diary

of

178 L. Trench Mortar Battery

September 1918.

To Headquarters,
178th Infantry Brigade

> HEADQUARTERS,
> 178th LIGHT TRENCH
> MORTAR BATTERY.
> No. C6/33
> Date. 2/9/1918

Herewith attached please
find War Diary for
September 1918 please

T. Harnett Capt
O.C. 178th LTMB

# WAR DIARY or INTELLIGENCE SUMMARY

September 1918

Army Form C. 2118.

175th L.T.M.B.

| Place | Date | Hour | Summary of Events and Information | Remarks and references to Appendices |
|---|---|---|---|---|
| CALONNE-SUR-LA-LYS | 1/9/18 | | Battery on salvage work | SHEET 36A S.E. |
| " | 2/9/18 | | Battery relieved 177th T.M.B. at Lestrem | LESTREM 36A S.E. |
| LESTREM | 3/9/18 | | One Rifle Section attached to 36th Bn. 'B' the Rifle action attached to 13th Bn. West Ridings & follow with them in the advance forward to the main ESTAIRES — LA-BASSÉE road | AUBERS 36A |
| " | 4/9/18 | | Battery H.Q. moved to M.7.B.3.2 | |
| " | 5/9/18 | | Two Rifle sections with forward Battalions moved to WANGERIE at M.17. B.7.3 and M.5.D.7.6 respectively | |
| LAVENTIE | 6/9/18 | | Headquarters moved to M.11. C. 5.6 | |
| " | 7/9/18 | 4.30 P.M. | Two guns in position covering Rifleman and Northumberland Avenues & Rotten Row 50 rounds fired at Latter trench | |
| " | 8/9/18 | 6 P.M. | Two guns took in position covering NAVY TRENCH — Guns registered | |
| " | 9/9/18 | 8 AM | 35 rounds fired on NAVY TRENCH | |
| " | " | 10.30 AM | " " Rifleman Avenue | |
| " | " | 10.30 AM | " " Rifleman Avenue | |
| " | 9/9/18 | midnight | Battery relieved by 177th L.T.M.B. Relief complete at 2.30 AM | |
| " | 10/9/18 | | Battery moved to M.14.B.8.8 Two guns with each Battalion sent to cover Corps near battle line | |
| " | 11/9 to 21/9/18 | | Battery training and building emplacements | |

J. Harnett Capt.

Army Form C. 2118.

# WAR DIARY
## or
## INTELLIGENCE SUMMARY.
(Erase heading not required.)

September 1918.   178th L.T.M.B.

Instructions regarding War Diaries and Intelligence Summaries are contained in F. S. Regs., Part II. and the Staff Manual respectively. Title pages will be prepared in manuscript.

| Place | Date | Hour | Summary of Events and Information | Remarks and references to Appendices |
|---|---|---|---|---|
| LAVANTIE | 22/9/18 | 10.15 pm | Battery relieved 177th L.T.M.B. in the line | MAP AUBERS 36 S.W.1. |
| " | 23/9/18 | 11.45 am | 25 rounds fired at N.1 D.7.6 | |
| | | 4.00 pm | 25 rounds fired at N.7 D.u.6.60 | |
| | | 7.00 pm | 35 rounds fired at N.19 A.2.8 | |
| | 24/9/18 25/9/18 | | Battery troops engaged in carrying parties | |
| | 26/9/18 | 11.05 am | 30 rounds fired on dugouts at N.1 D.9.2 | |
| | | 1.15 pm | 30 rounds fired in N.7 D.5.6 | |
| | | 3.00 pm | 35 rounds fired in trench N.13 D.4.2 | |
| | 27/9/18 | | 20 rounds fired on THE LOZENGE at N.19 A.9.4 | |
| | 28/9/18 | 3 am | 24 rounds fired on dugouts at N.19 A.89.65 | |
| | 29/9/18 | 2.30 am | 15 rounds fired on TWO TREE FARM | |
| | 30/9/18 | 7.30 am | Battery assisted 11th R.S.F. in the attack on enemy front system of trenches in front of AUBERS. | |

S. Hewett Capt.
Comdg 178 L.T.M.B.

Confidential

War Diary

of

178th Light Trench Mortar Battery

for

October 1918

To Headquarters
178th Infantry Brigade

> HEADQUARTERS,
> 178th LIGHT TRENCH
> MORTAR BATTERY.
>
> No. C8/22
> Date 3/10/18

Attached please find War
Diary for month of October
1918.

M Cowper Major Capt.
Cmdg 178th LTMB

VOLUME V

October 1918

Army Form C. 2118.

# WAR DIARY
## INTELLIGENCE SUMMARY.
(Erase heading not required.)

178<sup>nd</sup> Leigh't Trench Mortar Battery

| Place | Date | Hour | Summary of Events and Information | Remarks and references to Appendices |
|---|---|---|---|---|
| LAVENTIE | Sep 30 – Oct 1st 1918 | Midnight | Battery relieved by 177<sup>th</sup> L.T.M.B. and moved by march route to R.12.C.80.85. | SHEET 36 A |
| RIEZ BAILLEUL | 1/10/18 | – | Battery resting and cleaning up | |
| " | 2/10/18 | – | Battery moved by march route to BAC ST MAUR and relieved the 182<sup>nd</sup> L.T.M.B. in the left sector of the Divisional front. Headquarters at G.18.A.10.15. | SHEET 36 NW |
| ERQUINGHEM | 3/10/18 | – | 2 Guns attached to advance Battalion to assist them in the move forward. Battery Headquarters moved to H.8.B.30.25. | |
| " | 4/10/18 | – | 2 forward guns reached H.12.C.7.8. | |
| " | 5/10/18 | 1930 | Battery relieved by 176<sup>th</sup> L.T.M.B. forward teams being withdrawn to H.8.B.30.25. | |
| " | 6/10/18 | – | Baths under Battery arrangement. | |
| " | 7.8.9 & 10/10/18 | – | Battery training and fatigue work. | |
| BOIS GRENIER | 10/10/18 | – | Battery moved by march route to H.30.A.3.4. and relieved the 177<sup>th</sup> L.T.M.B. with four guns in U.C. line, covering outpost line of resistance | |
| " | " | – | Battery working on defensive emplacements | |
| " | 11, 12, 13, 14/10/18 | – | Four guns moved forward with their respective Battalions but were taken in the day withdrawn to MONT PINDO | |
| MONT PINDO | 16/10/18 | – | | |
| " | " | – | | |
| LOMME | 17/10/18 | – | Battery moved by march route to LOMME. Headquarters at J.28.D.5.6. | SHEET 36 NE |

Army Form C. 2118.

# WAR DIARY
# INTELLIGENCE SUMMARY

178th Light Trench Mortar Battery

October 1918

| Place | Date | Hour | Summary of Events and Information | Remarks and references to Appendices |
|---|---|---|---|---|
| MONT-EN-BARŒUL | 18/10/18 | | Battery moved by march route to MONS-EN-BARŒUL and billeted at FME DU HAUT | SHEET 36 NE |
| FOREST | 19/10/18 | | Battery moved by march route to FOREST and billeted at Chateau at G.35.C.0.1 | SHEET 37 |
| WILLEMS | 20/10/18 | | Battery moved by march route to WILLEMS and billeted in Brasserie | " |
| TEMPLEUVE | 21/10/18 | | Battery moved by march route to TEMPLEUVE and billeted at H.33.A.8.0 | " |
| " | 22–23 18/10/18 | | Battery clearing up. Baths under Battery arrangements | " |
| " | 24–6 31/10/18 | | Battery training | |

Hanns H Coft.

CONFIDENTIAL.

# WAR DIARY

OF

178th L. Trench Mortar Battery.

NOVEMBER, 1918.

Army Form C. 2118.

## VOLUME VI  NOVEMBER 1918  WAR DIARY

### INTELLIGENCE SUMMARY

178th L.T.M.B.

(Erase heading not required.)

| Place | Date | Hour | Summary of Events and Information | Remarks and references to Appendices |
|---|---|---|---|---|
| TEMPLEUVE | 1st to 7th | | Battery training | SHEET 37 H33 A8.0.7.H. |
| EPINETTE | 8th | 10·00 | Battery relieved 177th L.T.M.B. in the line. Headquarters at H.33.C.6.8. | " |
| FAUCHY | 9th | | Numbers 1 and 2 Sections moved forward to J17D1·7. Numbers 3 and 4 Sections with Battery H.Q. | " |
| " | " | | moved to REJ-DU-SART | " |
| ANVAING | 10th | | Numbers 1 and 2 Sections moved forward to ANVAING. Battery Headquarters moved to CORDES | " |
| " | 11th | 08·00 | Battery Headquarters and Numbers 3 and 4 Sections moved to ANVAING joining 1 and 2 Sections | " |
| " | " | | Hostilities cease at 11·00 | " |
| VELAINES | 12th | | Battery moved by march route to VELAINES. Battery Headquarters at K13C4·5 | " |
| " | 13th | | Battery cleaning up, improving billets, salvage | " |
| " | 14th | | Baths under Battery arrangements | " |
| PECQ | 15th | | Battery moved by march route to PECQ. Headquarters at I11B5·7 | " |
| WILLEMS | 16th | 11·00 | Battery moved by march route to WILLEMS. Billeted in houses at M5D7·0 | " |
| PETIT-RONCHIN | 17th | 09·00 | Battery moved by march route to PETIT-RONCHIN. Billeted at Q22 A3·3 | SHEET 36 |
| " | 18 | | Battery training and cleaning up | " |
| " | 19th | | Battery inspected by Brigadier General J.W. Stansfeld C.M.G. D.S.O. | " |
| " | 20 to 23 | | Battery training. Wheelers Rehans Clarkes | 7H. |

J. Howlett Capt. O.C.

VOLUME VI NOVEMBER 1918.

Army Form C. 2118.

WAR DIARY
or
~~INTELLIGENCE SUMMARY.~~
(Erase heading not required.)

178th L.T.M.B.

| Place | Date | Hour | Summary of Events and Information | Remarks and references to Appendices |
|---|---|---|---|---|
| PETIT RONCHIN | 24th | | Battery attended Church Parade on field at Q 28 A 4.1 | F.H. SHEET 36 |
| " | 25 | | Battery training. Bells under Battery arrangements | " " |
| " | 26 | | Battery attended Brigade parade when Ribands were presented to Officers and other Ranks | " " |
| " | | | by the Divisional Commander | " " |
| " | 27th to 30th | | Battery training, Education, Recreational Games etc in the afternoon | " F.H. |

H Harnett Capt.
C.C.

www.ingramcontent.com/pod-product-compliance
Lightning Source LLC
Chambersburg PA
CBHW081447160426
43193CB00013B/2402